An Adult Coloring Book Featuring Funny, F
Stress Relieving Designs for 50th Birthday

By © Neo coloration

ISBN-13: 979-8663404983

Thank you for purchasing this title, we hope you enjoy coloring this book! Neo Coloration is a young start-up dedicated to creating a variety of adult coloring books.

We love what we do and everyday we strive to improve our products to provide you with the best coloring experience. Your feedback is important as well if you have any, don't hesitate to contact us at neocoloration@mail.com

<u>Other titles you may like:</u>
Motivational Swear Word Coloring Book:
Do More of What Makes You F*cking Happy.
(ASIN B083XX25RZ)

Believe in Yourself:
An Adult Coloring Book Featuring Motivational
Sayings and Positive Affirmations.
(ASIN B084DGPN6N)

Without your voice, we don't exist.
Please support us and leave a review!
Thank you!

Coloring can enhance individuation and promote self-discovery de-stress and bring a sense of peace like a meditative exercise. Focusing on the lines of the pattern helps reduce stress and anxiety, stay present at the moment, easing anxiety about the past and worries about the future. besides getting a dose of humor and laughter that relaxes your whole body and decreases stress hormones etc...

Enjoy this snarky & relatable coloring book with each page you color.
This book contains 25 pages of funny and humorous fifty-year-old related designs and sayings surrounded with beautiful patterns, intricate details, mandalas, and flowers, etc...

Relax and enjoy some good vibes that will level up your confidence and will give you encouragement throughout the daily stress of life.

- Black background reverse pages to reduce bleed-through.
- Each page is single-sided for getting the best coloring experience.

Wishing you a fun-filled fabulous 50th!
Best wishes to you on this new and exciting chapter of your life!
may it be filled with fun, relaxation, adventure,
and anything you wish it to be.

2020 CLEARLY

DOESN'T COUNT SO

HAPPY 49th

BIRTHDAY AGAIN!

I'M NOT

50

I'M 30 WITH

20 years experience

50 **& I STILL LOVE TO PARTY**

AND BY "PARTY" I MEAN "TAKE NAPS"

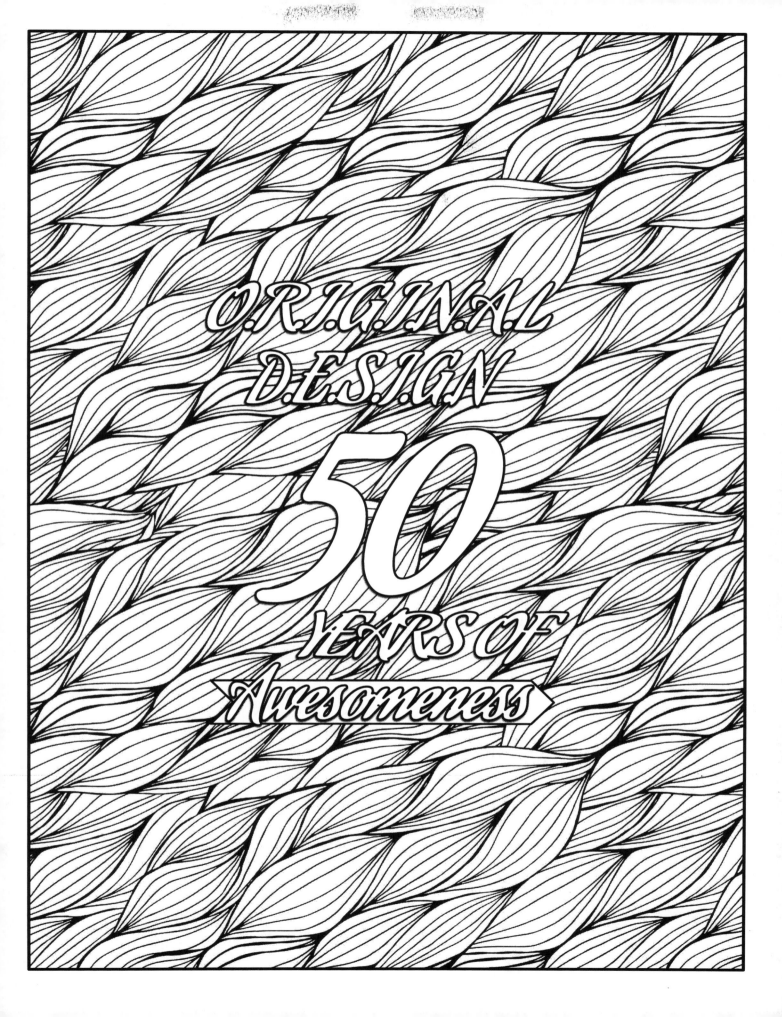

Color test page

Color test page